Volcano!

by Cynthia Pratt Nicolson

Kids Can Press

To my nana, Gladys Cockle

Acknowledgments

Many thanks go to Dr. Jennifer Getsinger, a geologist with the Geological Survey of Canada, for her careful and thorough checking of the draft manuscript for this book. Any errors that may have crept into the final book are my responsibility. I would also like to thank Val Wyatt and Stacey Roderick for editing with patience and good humor; Patricia Buckley for finding great photos; Julia Naimska for designing the book and the team at Kids Can Press for making this book possible.

Kids Can Press acknowledges the financial support of the Ontario Arts Council, the Canada Council for the Arts and the Government of Canada, through the BPIDP, for our publishing activity.

Published in Canada by
Kids Can Press Ltd.
29 Birch Avenue
Toronto, ON M4V 1E2

Published in the U.S. by
Kids Can Press Ltd.
2250 Military Road
Tonawanda, NY 14150

www.kidscanpress.com

Edited by Val Wyatt and Stacey Roderick
Designed by Julia Naimska
Printed and bound in Hong Kong by Book Art Inc., Toronto

The hardcover edition of this book is smyth sewn casebound.
The paperback edition of this book is limp sewn with a drawn-on cover.

CM 01 0 9 8 7 6 5 4 3 2 1
CM PA 01 0 9 8 7 6 5 4 3 2 1

Canadian Cataloguing in Publication Data

Nicolson, Cynthia Pratt
  Volcano!

(Disaster)
ISBN 1-55074-908-0 (bound)   ISBN 1-55074-966-8 (pbk.)
1. Volcanoes — Juvenile literature. I. Title. II. Series: Disaster (Toronto, Ont.).

QE521.3.N533 2001   j551.21   C00-933060-7

Photo Credits

Every reasonable effort has been made to trace ownership of and give accurate credit to copyrighted material. Information that would enable the publisher to correct any discrepancies in future editions would be appreciated.

Abbreviations
t = top; b = bottom; c = center; l = left; r = right
CVO = Cascades Volcano Observatory
HVO = Hawaii Volcano Observatory
USGS = United States Geological Survey

Cover photograph: Michael Doukas/United States Geological Survey/Cascades Volcano Observatory

p. 1: J.D. Griggs/USGS/HV0 (7-2-83); **p. 3:** (t) J.D. Griggs/USGS/HVO (3-13-85), (b) J.D. Griggs/USGS/HVO (3/28/83); **p. 4:** (t) J. Hughes/USDA Forest Service, (b) Harry Glicken/USGS/CVO; **p. 5:** Michael Doukas/USGS/CVO; **p. 6:** (t) UPI/ Corbis-Bettmann/Magma, (b) Daniel Dzurisin/ USGS/CV0; **p. 7:** (t) Volcano Watch International, (b) Lyn Topinka/ USGS/CVO; **p. 9:** (t) J.D. Griggs/USGS/CVO, (b) J. Nieland/ USDA Forest Service; **p. 10:** (t) Victor Last/Geographical Visual Aids, (b) National Geophysical Data Center/NOAA; **p. 11:** (t) J.D. Griggs/ USGS/HV0 (7-2-83), (b) National Parks Service/ Mount Rainer National Park; **p. 12:** (t) J.D. Griggs/USGS/HVO, (b) Chris Newhall/ USGS/CVO; **p. 13:** J.D. Griggs/USGS/HVO (3/13/85); **p. 14:** (t) UPI/ Corbis-Bettmann/Magma, (c) D.W. Peterson/USGS/HVO (3/27/84), (b) J.D. Griggs/USGS/HVO (11/84); **p. 15:** (l) C. Heliker/USGS/HVO (1-26-89), (r) HVO/USGS 133CP; **p. 16:** UPI/Corbis-Bettmann/ Magma; **p. 17:** (tl) Sean Sexton Collection/Corbis/Magma, (tr, b) Volcano Watch International; **p. 18:** Volcano Watch International; **p. 19:** (t) Volcano Watch International, (b) J.D. Griggs/USGS/HVO (11/26/86); **p. 20:** Library of Congress/LC-262-056433; **p. 21:** (t) Joe McDonald/ Tom Stack and Associates, (b) Library of Congress/Z62-25077; **p. 22:** Solarfilma; **p. 23:** (t) Solarfilma, (b) Courtesy Richard S. Williams/ USGS; **p. 24:** Jeff Marso/USGS/CVO; **p. 25:** (t) Reuters/Bob Strong/ Archive Photos, (b) Olga Lucia Jordan/International Federation; **p. 26:** J.D. Griggs/USGS/HVO (3-28-83); **p. 27:** (t) USGS/CVO, (b) C. Heliker/ USGS/HVO (12/11/92); **p. 28:** USGS/CVO; **p. 29:** (t) Chris Newhall/ USGS/CVO, (b) Reuters/Corbis-Bettmann/Magma; **p. 30:** Lyn Topinka/ USGS/CVO.

CONTENTS

"THIS IS IT!"

May 18, 1980, dawned bright and sunny in Washington state. Birds sang in the trees near David Johnston's campsite on a ridge 8 km (5 mi.) from Mount St. Helens' peak.

The thirty-year-old scientist was there to monitor the volcano. For two months, he and other volcanologists (scientists who study volcanoes) had been concerned about Mount St. Helens. They knew that rising magma (melted rock) was causing the mountain's north face to bulge outward. Sooner or later, the volcano would erupt.

Johnston was aware of the danger. He had warned others to leave the area while he stayed to keep watch.

For 123 years, Mount St. Helens rested peacefully. Then, in the spring of 1980, it began to stir. Magma surged up through channels inside the mountain. Beneath its snowy slopes, the volcano was seething.

As the sun rose, the snowy mountain looked exactly as it had the day before. But at 8:32 A.M., the swollen north face broke away and began to slide downhill. Johnston rushed to call his headquarters in Vancouver, Washington. This was the moment he had been waiting for. Mount St. Helens was erupting!

"Vancouver! Vancouver! This is it!" David Johnston's final radio message announced that Mount St. Helens had blown its stack. An avalanche of rocks, ice, snow and soil crashed down the mountainside. Ash billowed into the sky, much as it did during another eruption later the same year, shown here from the south.

Volcanologist David Johnston recorded the volcano's warning signs. When Mount St. Helens erupted, a blast of hot rocks, dust and gases swept through Johnston's campsite at more than 300 km/h (200 m.p.h.), killing him instantly. Fifty-six other people also died during the eruption.

WN VOLCANO

kyard! All you need are the materials in this kit,
nge food color, and dishwashing liquid.

3. In the cup, mix one spoonful of water, one spoonful of
baking soda, two drops of food coloring, and a small squeeze
of dishwashing liquid.

4. Pour the contents into the test tube and watch the volcano erupt!

*When the baking soda from this kit runs
out, ask an adult to get you more.
If you don't have any at home, you can
purchase some at the grocery store.*

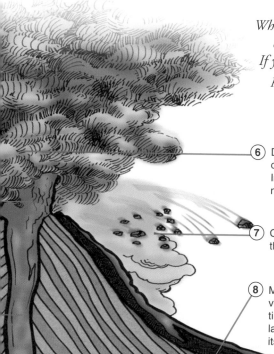

6 During an eruption, steam, ash, and gas pour
out of the volcano and rise high into the sky.
In the most violent eruptions, ash can rise
more than 20 miles (32 km) high.

7 Chunks of lava, called *bombs*, fly out of
the crater.

8 Molten lava flows down the sides of the
volcano, where it cools and hardens. Over
time, numerous eruptions build layer upon
layer of hardened lava, giving the volcano
its distinctive cone shape.

1 Boiling-hot magma deep inside the earth bubbles and
oozes upward. It gathers below the volcano in a large pool
called a *magma chamber*, where it mixes with gas and water.

WITH THIS KIT, you can create your own volcanic eruption. The eruption is the result of a basic chemical reaction. When vinegar (an acid) and the "lava powder," which is baking soda (a base), are mixed together, they react violently and produce carbon dioxide bubbles, or in this case, "lava." The bubbles rise out of the volcano and flow down the sides. You will be adding dishwashing liquid to slow the reaction somewhat, making the eruption last longer.

You can make the volcano erupt as many times as you want, because vinegar and baking soda are common items found around your home.

PAINTING THE VOLCANO

This kit includes two colors of paint and a brush to paint your plastic volcano. Use the illustration on the right as a painting guide.

GET OUT...

There are two types of lava, *aa* (pronounced ah-ah) and *pahoehoe* (pronounced pa-HOY-hoy) that flow out of a volcano. Aa lava moves slowly and dries to form sharp, jagged rock. Pahoehoe lava is runny and flows very quickly. It forms smooth, ropelike coils when it cools.

AND STAY OUT!

When magma is sticky and rocklike, it is called *tephra*. Here are the five types and sizes of tephra that are ejected from a volcano.

NAME	SIZE
Dust	0.01 inch (.25 mm) or less
Ash	0.01 to 0.1 inches (.25 to 2 mm)
Lapilli	0.1 inches to 2.5 inches (2 to 64 mm)
Blocks (hard lava)	2.5 inches (64 mm) and larger
Bombs (soft lava)	2.5 inches (64 mm) and larger

Written by Raymond Miller
Illustrated by Dan Jankowski
© 2002 Pace Products, Inc.
333 Semoran Commerce Place, Apopka, FL 32703

Printed in USA
Item# 22012
1 3 5 7 9 10 8 6 4 2

FORCES OF DESTRUCTION

The landslide on the north face of Mount St. Helens triggered a reign of destruction that lasted all day. The volcano was blowing its stack.

The avalanche of ice, snow, rock and other debris roared down the mountain and into the surrounding countryside. It choked the Toutle River with mounds of rock and gravel for 23 km (14 mi.).

The avalanche released built-up pressure inside the mountain, and the volcano exploded. A hot blast of gases, dust and rock, called a pyroclastic surge, shot out sideways and upward. The blast created a stone-filled wind that shot down the mountain, knocking down huge trees in a vast area. When the surge slammed into Spirit Lake, the water rose and then

A photographer's car 16 km (10 mi.) away from the summit was buried in ash. A heavy coating of ash colored everything a ghostly gray. Some of the ash mixed with melted snow and ice and turned into flowing mud as thick as wet cement.

fell again, pulling hundreds of the blown-down trees into the lake.

A cloud of ash 24 km (15 mi.) high poured from the volcano's summit. It continued to billow out for nine hours. The ash drifted eastward, blanketing much of Washington and neighboring states in gritty, gray powder that clogged car motors and made breathing difficult. Falling ash melted snow and ice on the mountaintop, producing cement-like mudflows, called lahars. Roads, bridges and logging camps were wiped out by the raging rivers of mud.

Breathing through a face mask, nine-year-old Jeff Trickey makes a call from an ash-coated phone booth.

After a landslide, explosion, ash cloud and mudflow, you might think the eruption was over. But Mount St. Helens wasn't ready to quit. Later in the afternoon, it belched out a scorching stream of gas-filled rock and ash called a pyroclastic flow. This bubbling material eventually hardened to form a smooth "pumice plain" at the base of the mountain.

By dusk, the land around Mount St. Helens was transformed beyond recognition. Lush green forest was now lifeless, gray wasteland. The eruption had lopped 396 m (1300 ft.) off the top of the mountain, and a gaping crater replaced the once-beautiful snowcapped cone.

Thousands of birds, deer, elk and fish were killed by the eruption. Some small animals, like this ground squirrel, hid in burrows and ate roots and bulbs to stay alive. By mixing ash and nutrients into the soil, these animals helped prepare the way for plants to return.

DISASTER DATA

Volcanoes are powerful. Some spew molten lava that buries houses and farms. Others belch car-sized lumps of solid rock. Volcanoes can also blast out deadly mixtures of hot ash, rock and gas or trigger wild floods of mud. In the past 400 years, volcanoes have killed nearly 300 000 men, women and children. Around the world, people are asking, "Can we stop these disasters?"

Huge trees toppled like toothpicks in the surge of hot gas, rocks and ash that blasted from the erupting Mount St. Helens. More than 24 000 ha (60 000 acres) of forest were flattened — enough lumber to build 150 000 houses. The two scientists in this photo are dwarfed by the destruction.

Fire from THE DEEP

Volcanoes reveal Earth's hidden secret: our planet is not as cool as it seems. In fact, the deeper you go, the hotter it gets.

Earth has four main layers: the inner core, outer core, mantle and crust. Volcanoes are formed when heat from the core and mantle causes melted rock to bubble up through the crust. This molten rock, called magma, rises because it is less dense than the surrounding rocks. Once it bursts onto Earth's surface, the molten rock is called lava. A volcano is any place where lava emerges from the ground.

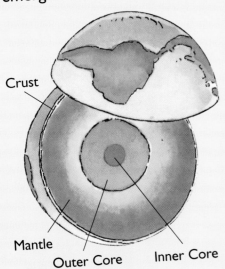

Crust

Mantle

Outer Core   Inner Core

DISASTER DATA

An *active* volcano is busy erupting — or giving signs that it might erupt soon. A *dormant* volcano seems to be sleeping, but it could erupt some time in the future. An *extinct* volcano is one that probably will never erupt again.

There are three different types of volcanoes, each with its own shape.
• Explosive eruptions form tall, steep-sided mountains called **composite volcanoes** or stratovolcanoes. Sticky, bubble-filled magma squeezes up into underground chambers. If the vents leading from the chambers become blocked by solidified lava, pressure builds. Finally, the volcano explodes, shattering the lava into tiny particles of volcanic ash. In later eruptions, liquid lava flows down the mountainsides. Alternating layers of ash and lava build up eruption after eruption, forming a large cone-shaped mountain.
• Explosive eruptions sometimes produce small volcanoes called **cinder cones**. These smooth-sided mountains are made of ash and loose bits of rock.
• Oozing lava forms broad, flat mounds called **shield volcanoes**. These free-flowing volcanoes cover a wide area and often have many side vents.

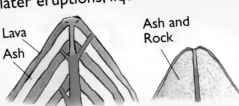

Lava
Ash

Composite Volcano

Ash and Rock

Cinder Cone

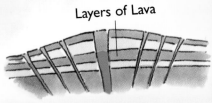

Layers of Lava

Shield Volcano

A fountain of lava spurts skyward from Kilauea, a shield volcano on the island of Hawaii. Hardened lava forms the black slopes of this large volcano, which has been active since it formed more than 300 000 years ago. In recent years, Kilauea has burned trees, buried dozens of houses and covered long stretches of highway with black lava rock.

Ape Cave was formed during a lava eruption from Mount St. Helens, a composite volcano. Flowing lava sometimes cools and hardens on the outside while staying bubbling hot inside. Eventually, the molten lava drains away, leaving a hollow tunnel called a lava tube. Composite volcanoes like Mount St. Helens alternate between lava flows and explosive, ash-producing eruptions.

YOU TRY IT

To see how magma rises inside the Earth, take a large, wide-necked jar and fill it with cold water. Fill a small bottle with very hot water to which you have added a few drops of red food coloring. Carefully lower the small bottle into the large jar so that it doesn't spill. Watch what happens. Because hot water is less dense than cold water, it rises through the cold water around it. In much the same way, red-hot magma rises through colder, denser rock in Earth's crust.

ERUPTION ZONE!

Do you live near a volcano? About one-tenth of the world's population does. Volcanoes aren't spread evenly over the Earth. Instead, they are concentrated in a few places. To understand why, check out our planet's crust.

Though it seems solid when we walk on it, Earth's outer crust is broken into about twenty large chunks called tectonic plates. These slabs of solid rock float on the softer, hotter rock of the mantle underneath. Currents in the mantle drag the crustal plates, causing them to pull apart, collide and scrape past each other. Although the plates move very slowly — at about the speed your fingernails grow — the power of their collisions is enormous.

Volcanoes form in the following three places:
• at **rift zones**, where two tectonic plates pull apart
• over **hot spots** in the middle of tectonic plates
• at **subduction zones**, where one tectonic plate plunges under another

Steaming geysers shoot up from the ground in Iceland. This island country sits on a rift zone where two plates pull apart under the Atlantic Ocean. As the plates slowly separate, magma squeezes up between them, triggering earthquakes, geysers and volcanoes. Undersea rift zones have produced volcanic ridges that circle the Earth like the seams on a baseball.

Earth's tectonic plates are outlined in yellow on this computer-generated image. Can you find the rift zone snaking down the middle of the Atlantic Ocean floor? How about the loop of plate boundaries surrounding the Pacific Ocean? Most of the world's 600 active volcanoes sizzle and fume on this loop, giving it the nickname "Ring of Fire."

Creeping lava ignores a stop sign on the island of Hawaii. The whole chain of Hawaiian islands has formed above a hot spot — a plume of hot rock rising from Earth's mantle. As the Pacific plate moves across this spot, the heat burns through, like a blowtorch piercing a sheet of metal.

Washington's Mount Rainier looks peaceful, but beware! It is above a subduction zone that extends along the west coast of Canada and the United States. Here, the Juan de Fuca plate dives under the North American plate. Scientists watch Mount Rainier and wonder, will this volcano erupt like its "sister," Mount St. Helens?

Out of the MONSTER'S MOUTH

Volcanoes are like belching monsters, spewing rocks, ash, gas and lava. What comes out depends on what's going on inside. How hot and bubbly is the magma? How much pressure has built up? Because a volcano's output may change from one eruption to the next, even the experts can be surprised. When a volcano opens its mouth, look out below!

Like thick chocolate syrup, lava pours across a field. Lava that forms a smooth or ropy surface like this is known by the Hawaiian name pahoehoe (pa-hoy-hoy). Lava that cools into rough, sharp chunks is called aa (ah-ah), which is just what you might say if you tried to walk on it.

A Filipino miner holds a chunk of pumice from Mount Pinatubo. Pumice is formed when lava cools and hardens with lots of air bubbles trapped inside. This rock is so light it floats!

An emergency helicopter flies over a soaring lava fountain in Hawaii. Thin, watery lava flows smoothly, while sticky, gas-filled lava spurts out. Fresh lava is extremely hot, between 700°C and 1500°C (1300°F and 2700°F). It cools to form solid rock.

A gas mask and ski goggles protect a Spokane, Washington, resident as he sweeps ash from his car after the eruption of Mount St. Helens. Explosive volcanoes often erupt with such a blast that their shattered lava turns to powder. If the ash and dust particles reach high into the atmosphere, they can be carried around the world.

DISASTER DATA

Ash spewed high into the atmosphere from an erupting volcano can travel great distances and even affect the weather. In 1815, ash from Indonesia's Tambora volcano caused strange sunsets and low temperatures around the world. The following year was so cold because of ash in the atmosphere that people called it "the year without a summer." Some farmers as far away as the United States found snow on their fields and frozen crops — in July!

Liquid lava can form small blobs as it falls to the ground. Hawaiians call these droplets "Pele's tears." (Pele is the Hawaiian volcano goddess.)

Lava sometimes stretches into thin, glassy threads as it flies through the air. In Hawaii, golden strands like these are called "Pele's hair."

A scientist inspects a volcanic block — a chunk of solid rock thrown from a volcano. Blocks can be as big as a car, or even a house.

Volcanic bombs are chunks of lava that cool and harden as they fall through the air. Most are slightly rounded and about the size of a tennis ball, but some can be bigger than a football. Air rushing past a falling bomb can create grooves in its surface. These make a whistling sound as the bomb drops.

YOU TRY IT

Here's a quick way to make a mini-volcano. Take a small juice bottle and scrunch aluminum foil around it to create a cone shape. Leave the bottle open at the top. Set the bottle on a large roasting pan, and use a funnel to put 10 mL (2 tsp.) of baking

powder into it. Then mix 125 mL (¹/₂ c.) of vinegar, a few drops of red food coloring and a squirt of liquid dish soap together in a measuring cup. Stir gently. Pour the vinegar mixture into the bottle. Stand by and admire as your mini-volcano gushes freely.

When Time STOOD STILL

People in the Roman town of Pompeii were puzzled when they awoke on the morning of August 24, A.D. 79. Why was the sky so dark?

Stepping outside, they found their answer. Fine ash was falling on the streets and buildings. There was so much of it that it blocked the sun. Mount Vesuvius had slumbered peacefully near the town for 800 years. But now it was erupting!

Chunks of rock began to rain down. The air smelled like rotten eggs.

People were confused. Should they hide indoors — or run for their lives?

Some fled to the harbor and climbed into boats. Others hid in cellars or struggled to gather their possessions and pets. Suddenly, the mountain blasted out an avalanche of super-hot gas and ash. Those who had stayed behind were killed instantly as scorching hot air filled their lungs and burned their skin. Over the next few hours, Pompeii was completely buried beneath volcanic ash. The grisly scene would lie undisturbed for nearly 1800 years.

Then, in 1860, an archaeologist named Guiseppe Fiorelli began to excavate Pompeii. His crew discovered hollow cavities in the exact shapes of people and animals — those who died during the eruption of Mount Vesuvius. The workers filled the holes with plaster to make replicas of the volcano's victims.

In 1961, archaeologists dug through the compacted ash where the town of Pompeii once stood. Like earlier teams, they found holes containing bones. These bones were the only remains of the victims of Mount Vesuvius's eruption. The holes were filled with plaster, to create casts of the victims' bodies.

A dog died chained to a post when Mount Vesuvius erupted. This plaster cast of its body shows how the dog struggled to get away. People were not the only victims of Mount Vesuvius.

Plaster casts show a mother and child huddled together, overcome by scorching gas and ash from Mount Vesuvius.

DISASTER DATA

The A.D. 79 eruption of Mount Vesuvius is probably the world's most famous volcanic event. But it's far from being the most deadly. Here's how Vesuvius compares with other killer volcanoes.

Volcano	Date	Deaths
Vesuvius, Italy	A.D. 79	2 000
Tambora, Indonesia	1815	92 000
Krakatoa, Indonesia	1883	36 000
Pelée, Martinique	1902	29 000
Ruiz, Colombia	1985	25 000

Today, trees grow in the ruins of Pompeii. Mount Vesuvius has been dormant since 1944, but scientists now worry that it may be starting to stir. More than two million people live in the shadow of this famous killer.

Hot Temper or HOT SPOT?

Hawaii's lush green islands have a violent past. Local legends blame it on Pele, the Hawaiian volcano goddess. They say that Pele created the islands during fights with her sister, the goddess of the sea. According to legend, Pele still dwells on the Big Island of Hawaii. When Pele is angry, the volcano Kilauea erupts.

Scientists explain that the Hawaiian islands formed over a hot spot, a plume of hot rock rising from Earth's mantle. As the Pacific plate glides westward, it travels over the hot spot. Magma rises through the ocean floor, and a volcanic island forms. When the plate moves, the magma creates another volcano. One by one, Hawaii's islands have risen from the depths.

Kauai and Oahu were the first two islands to appear above sea level. Their hills have been rounded and worn by wind and rain, and they have no active volcanoes. The Big Island of Hawaii is now above the hot spot. It has two active volcanoes: Mauna Loa and Kilauea.

Like a glowing space alien, fresh lava creeps across older volcanic rock. Although its front edge advances more slowly than you walk, lava is dangerous. It picks up speed when it flows through channels or down steep slopes. Where lava meets the sea and hardens, the new land it forms can collapse into the ocean without warning.

Beneath the ocean waves east of the Big Island, a new volcano is growing. Called Loihi, it may eventually become a new island in the chain. One thing is certain. Without volcanic activity, the Hawaiian islands wouldn't exist.

Nature puts on a fireworks display in the night sky over Kilauea. Molten lumps of rock called lava bombs leave trails of steam and smoke as they fly from the volcano's glowing mouth.

Red-hot lava sets fire to trees and houses on the Big Island as the volcano Kilauea erupts yet again. Since 1983, the volcano has destroyed 181 homes and added 205 ha (507 acres) of new land to the island's shore. Mauna Loa, the island's other active volcano, is the largest mountain in the world. Measured from its base on the sea floor, it is taller than Mount Everest.

YOU TRY IT

Make a quick model of the slow process that created the Hawaiian islands. Cut out the center of a foam meat tray. Wrap aluminum foil across this frame and secure it around the edges. Ask a friend to hold a pencil, point up, in one spot. Slowly move the foil plate above the pencil tip. As you do this, your friend should raise and lower the pencil, poking through the plate six times. In the same way the pencil pierces the foil plate,

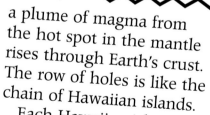

a plume of magma from the hot spot in the mantle rises through Earth's crust. The row of holes is like the chain of Hawaiian islands. Each Hawaiian island is the tip of an underwater volcano. The chain formed as the Pacific plate glided over a hot spot in Earth's crust.

19

WEIRD WARNINGS

On May 5, 1902, dozens of poisonous snakes invaded the town of St. Pierre on the Caribbean island of Martinique. The snakes were fleeing from the trembling slopes of Mount Pelée, a nearby volcano. Then a torrent of watery mud rushed down the mountain and killed twenty-four people.

At first, the residents of St. Pierre ignored the danger signals. They were preparing for an election on May 10, and no one wanted to miss the big event.

A visitor surveys the ruins of St. Pierre on the Caribbean island of Martinique. The town was obliterated when a pyroclastic flow (fast-moving wind of super-hot gas and ash) roared down from nearby Mount Pelée.

Over the next two days, clouds of black smoke and ash erupted from Mount Pelée. On the morning of May 8, the town was cloaked in darkness. People decided to leave. But it was too late. At 7:50 A.M., the volcano exploded with a thundering boom. A dark purple cloud of searing gases sped down its slopes. Within two minutes, the whole town of St. Pierre disappeared. All but two of its 30 000 residents were killed instantly.

Three days before the eruption of Mount Pelée, dozens of pit vipers like this one left the rumbling mountain and slithered into the town of St. Pierre. They swarmed the streets and killed more than 200 animals and 50 humans with their poisonous bites.

Mount Pelée looms above the shattered walls of St. Pierre. On the morning of May 8, 1902, the volcano took the lives of 30 000 people in just a few minutes.

YOU TRY IT

Volcanoes like Mount Pelée explode when gas-filled magma is suddenly released from underground. You can model this process with a bottle of pop. (Make sure you do this activity outside or over a sink.) Shake the bottle gently and notice the bubbles of carbon dioxide gas inside. Now shake more vigorously. Like a volcano, your pop bottle is under intense pressure. Point it away from you while you quickly unscrew the cap and watch the "pyroclastic flow" spurt out.

Battling a VOLCANO

Imagine watching your home disappear under a mound of hardened black lava. That's what happened to many families on the Icelandic island of Heimaey in 1973.

Very early on the morning of January 23, some of Heimaey's residents were woken by a red glow in the sky. At first, they thought a house was on fire. But as the glow grew, they realized it was coming right out of the ground. Just outside town, red-hot lava and ash were rising as high as a fifty-story building.

As the lava fell to the ground, it piled up, forming a cone-shaped mountain. Then it began creeping toward the town. Emergency crews roused the town's sleeping residents. Most of the islanders were loaded

On Heimaey, an Icelandic island, houses collapsed under the weight of the volcanic ash and rock. Others caught fire when they were hit by glowing lava bombs. Remarkably, no lives were lost during the eruption.

into small boats and sent to safety on the mainland. About 300 stayed behind, determined to save their town. But how?

Islanders pumped seawater through firehoses to stop the advancing lava. In a battle that lasted five months, the volunteer volcano fighters used 43 pumps and over 30 km (19 mi.) of pipe and hose. About 400 buildings were buried during the eruption, but the town's harbor was saved.

The rough, clinking lava rock crept closer, burying several homes and threatening to choke off the island's precious harbor. Then a scientist had an idea. Perhaps cold water would stop the lava.

The volcano-fighters pumped seawater through firehoses to spray the lava. At first, the water seemed to have no effect. The lava kept advancing. It began to form a wall across the harbor entrance. But the islanders did not give up. They continued to spray until finally, after an amazing five months, the lava flow stopped. With its new, narrower entrance, the harbor was safer than ever before!

DISASTER DATA

Iceland is sitting in an awkward spot — in a rift zone, right where two of Earth's crustal plates are moving apart. As the North American plate heads west and the European plate heads east, they open a crack in the sea floor. Magma from deep inside the Earth rises up through this crack, producing a ridge of undersea volcanoes. Iceland and its smaller neighbors are the tips of such volcanoes.

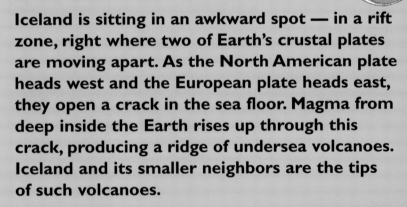

Like a science-fiction monster, lava invaded Heimaey's buildings and streets. When it was finally halted in early July, one-fifth of the town was buried. Many residents have now returned to Heimaey. Like many other Icelanders, they use volcanic underground heat (geothermal energy) to produce steam heat to warm their homes.

A Torrent OF MUD

For over a year, Nevado del Ruiz had been rumbling. Volcanologists warned officials in the town of Armero, Colombia, that the nearby volcano could erupt at any time. But the warnings were brushed aside. The officials didn't want to disturb people with a false alarm. When they finally took action, it was too late.

A few trees managed to survive when the town of Armero, Colombia, was swept away. The Ruiz volcano sent a river of mud hurtling through the town at speeds of up to 35 km/h (20 m.p.h.).

Nevado del Ruiz erupted on November 13, 1985. It spewed hot ash and gas over the icecap at its peak, melting the ice and triggering an instant flood. A wall of water swept into the Lagunillas River. It quickly mixed with mud to form a lahar, a flowing mixture like wet cement.

Two hours after the eruption, a 40 m (130 ft.) high wave of water and mud hit Armero. The town was washed away.

About 25 000 people were killed. Another 5000 were injured and 10 000 were left homeless. Although its eruption was only one-tenth the size of Mount St. Helens, Ruiz was the most devastating volcano of the twentieth century.

A mud-covered woman is carried to safety after being rescued from Armero by helicopter. Within four hours of the eruption, the town was buried up to 5 m (15 ft.) deep in a concrete-like mixture of water, ash and mud.

Red Cross volunteers work with children in an emergency camp for Ruiz survivors. Many children lost their homes and families in the disaster. Colombia called on international aid to help the survivors.

FACING DANGER
to Save Lives

Approaching a dormant volcano is like sneaking up on a sleeping lion. You don't know when it will snarl. That doesn't stop curious volcanologists from reaching right into the gaping mouths of volcanoes around the world.

Volcanologists often work in labs and offices. But to collect new data, they need to visit volcanoes. Some volcanologists climb steep mountains to place earthquake-measuring devices on trembling slopes. Others crawl into seething craters to collect rock and gas samples.

Using a metal shield for protection, a volcanologist probes a scorching lava flow. Volcanologists use special thermometers called thermocouples to take the temperature of lava flows. Regular glass thermometers would melt in the 1100°C (2000°F) heat.

An ox cart carries a team of volcanologists into a flooded area in the Philippines. Volcanologists often need to travel to hard-to-get-to places where an eruption has just occurred.

Why do scientists take such risks? Because they want to know how volcanoes work. With better understanding, volcanologists can make more accurate predictions. By warning people of danger, they hope to save lives.

A volcanologist takes samples of gases trapped beneath the surface of hardened lava. She wears a face mask to avoid breathing the toxic fumes. By analyzing a volcano's gases, scientists can sometimes predict changes in its activity.

YOU TRY IT

"Why did you become a volcanologist?" "What's the scariest thing that ever happened to you?" Visit the Volcano World Internet site to find out how several scientists answered these questions. For interviews with volcanologists and the latest news about volcanoes, go to:
http://volcano.und.nodak.edu

A Giant WAKES UP

Mount Pinatubo was twitching. For nearly 600 years, the huge Philippine volcano had lain quiet and still. Then, in April 1991, it began to stir.

Native people living on Pinatubo's green slopes felt the ground tremble beneath their feet. They noticed steam spurting from cracks in the rocks and a smell of rotten eggs in the air. So they called in the volcano experts.

The volcanologists checked Mount Pinatubo and decided that it was about to erupt.

They showed people a video of previous eruptions to warn them of the dangers. "Move out," they said, "before it's too late." Most people heeded the warning and left quickly.

A severe tropical storm brought heavy rains during Mount Pinatubo's eruption. Mudflows called lahars ruined many communities and hundreds of farms. The lahars continued long after the volcano stopped erupting. They are still a threat today.

Floods forced these boys onto a rooftop. They were rescued just after this picture was taken.

On June 12, strong eruptions began to blast ash from the volcano's summit. Then, on the morning of June 15, Mount Pinatubo exploded with a mighty roar.

The eruption killed about 350 people who had stayed in the danger zone. But Pinatubo's death toll could have been much, much worse. The volcanologists' warnings saved about 50 000 lives.

A thick, heavy blanket of ash from Mount Pinatubo covered buildings, cars and roads. Many farmers' crops were destroyed by the volcano. Though it looks like gray snow, ash doesn't melt. It needs to be shoveled up and carried away.

Living
IN THE SHADOW

In spite of the danger, people continue to live near many of Earth's most violent volcanoes. Why?

Many people cannot afford to move away from dangerous volcanoes. Others forget that familiar mountains can also be killers. They may not believe that a long-dormant volcano will ever erupt again.

Some stay because the land is excellent for farming. Volcanic ash adds nutrients to soil. The grape-growing fields of Sicily, Italy, for instance, have been enriched by ash from nearby Mount Etna.

Volcanoes also provide magnificent scenery and space for wilderness adventure. Washington's Mount Rainier (shown below) is popular with skiers and snowboarders.

Volcanoes remind us of nature's power. No one can stop a volcano, but with new instruments and knowledge, volcanologists are learning to make more accurate predictions. If people listen to their warnings, many lives will be saved.

Glossary

Aa: lava that has cooled into rough, sharp chunks

Ash: tiny fragments of rock and lava that spew into the air like fine powder when a volcano explodes

Cinder cone: a small volcano formed from ash and loose bits of rock produced during an explosive volcanic eruption. Cinder cones are often formed on the sides of larger volcanoes.

Composite volcano: a volcano, like Mount St. Helens, that is built up from alternating eruptions of ash and lava. Composite volcanoes are also called stratovolcanoes.

Core: the center portion of the Earth

Crust: the solid outer layer of the Earth

Geologist: a scientist who studies the Earth

Geothermal energy: heat produced by Earth's interior

Geyser: a natural fountain of hot water and steam that spurts up into the air. The water is heated inside the Earth.

Hot spot: the area above a plume of hot rock rising from Earth's mantle

Lahar: a mudflow produced when ice and snow are melted and mixed with ash during a volcanic eruption

Lava: melted rock on Earth's surface

Lava tube: a hollow tunnel formed when lava drains away beneath an outer surface of lava that has already cooled and hardened.

Magma: melted rock inside the Earth

Mantle: the middle layer of Earth's interior

Pahoehoe: lava that cools to form a smooth or ropy surface

Pumice: bubble-filled volcanic rock. Some pumice is so light, it floats.

Pyroclastic flow: a ground-hugging stream of bubble-filled rock and ash released from a volcano

Pyroclastic surge: an air-borne blast of hot gases, dust and rock released by a volcano

Rift: a split between tectonic plates that are moving apart

Shield volcano: a broad, flat mountain built up by eruptions of free-flowing lava

Stratovolcano: see composite volcano

Subduction zone: an area where one tectonic plate dives under another

Tectonic plates: slabs of Earth's crust and upper mantle layer

Volcanic blocks: solid chunks of rock thrown into the air by a volcano

Volcanic bombs: chunks of lava spewed into the air. Bombs cool and harden as they fall to the ground.

Volcano: any place where melted rock emerges through Earth's crust

Volcanologist: a scientist who studies volcanoes

Index